D0903945

TOY THEATERS

Lyndie Wright

Consultant: Henry Pluckrose

Photography: Chris Fairclough

FRANKLIN WATTS
New York/London/Sydney/Toronto

Copyright © 1991 Franklin Watts

Franklin Watts, Inc.
387 Park Avenue South
New York, N.Y. 10016

Library of Congress Cataloging-in-Publication Data

Wright, Lyndie.
    Toy theaters / Lyndie Wright.
        p.   cm. — (Fresh start)
    Summary: Describes how to construct and use a variety of toy
theaters, including spinning-disk theaters, Punch and Judy theaters,
shadow theaters, and Victorian toy theaters.
    ISBN 0-531-14196-9
    1. Toy theaters—Models—Juvenile literature.   [1. Toy theaters.
2. Models and modelmaking.]   I. Title.   II. Series: Fresh start
(London, England)
PN1979.T6W7 1991
791.5—dc20   90-31636
                                                          CIP AC

Design: K and Co

Editor: Jenny Wood

Typeset by Lineage Ltd,
Watford, England

Printed in Belgium

Contents

This book describes activities which use the following:

Adhesives (White glue, clear glue, Pritt Glue Stick)

Fun-Tac

Brass paper fasteners

Brushes (for glue and paint)

Cardboard (thin and thick, white and black, 8½ x 11in and 11 x 17in)

Cardboard boxes (for example, shoe boxes)

Cellophane (colored)

Theater Gel Color Filters (an alternative to colored cellophane, these are nonflammable filters for theater lights)

Compasses (for drawing circles)

Crayons

Feathers

Dowel rods (wood) or skewer sticks

Hole punch

India inks

Masking tape

Metallic paper (for example, candy wrappers)

Paint (poster or tempera)

Paper (thin and thick, white and black, 8½ x 11in and 11 x 17in)

Paper clips

Pencils

Pens – felt-tipped
— gold and/or silver metallic ink pens

Pliers

Reading lamp (or flashlight)

Ruler

Scissors

Sequins

Tissue paper

Trimming knife

Wire

1 Some of the materials you will need when making the toy theaters in this book.

Making toy theaters, and the scenery and figures to go inside them, is fun and inexpensive. The basic materials for the theaters described in this book are paper, cardboard, cardboard boxes and paints. The only things you may need to buy are glue, paper fasteners, cellophane or colored gel filters (see page 45), wooden dowels and metallic ink pens. Keep the wrappers from candy and gum to use as decoration on some of the booths and figures, and collect some feathers and sequins for decoration, too.

Before you start your adventure into making toy theaters, make sure you have a good-sized work area available. Cover this with newspaper, especially when using glue and paints.

When you are ready to make scenery and characters for your toy theater, think about the story you want to base your show on. You might like to write your own play or adapt a fairy tale or legend. You may prefer to follow a playscript in a book. Remember to keep the characters' speeches short, so that they do not have to stand still on the stage for too long. Be careful to move only the figure which is talking, so that your audience knows which character is speaking.

When you have experimented with the ideas in this book, try to use the techniques to develop new theater and figure designs of your own.

Christmas crib figures made from paper cut-outs were used in the 17th century and were probably the forerunners of toy theater.

To make your own crib you will need a sheet of thick paper or thin cardboard (11 x 17in in size), a pencil, scissors, a ruler, paints and paintbrushes (or inks, felt-tipped pens or crayons), and glue.

1 Fold the sheet of paper or cardboard in half.

2 Lay the folded paper or cardboard on your work surface, with the fold facing towards you. Draw a picture of the outside of the stable on the front. Make a large stable opening. If there is enough room around the opening, draw the Three Kings and some shepherds.

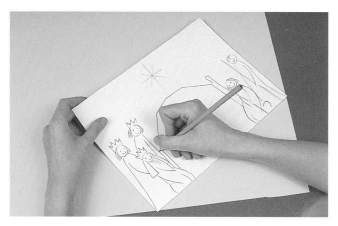

3 Cut out the opening, keeping the cut-out piece intact.

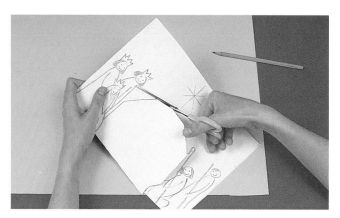

4 Unfold the paper or cardboard and, on the reverse, draw a line about 2in away from the opening.

5 Make a fold along this line using the edge of the ruler.

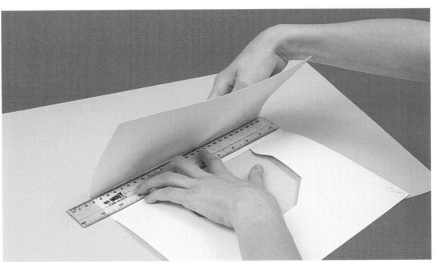

6 Go back to your picture of the stable and cut away the top corners to make a roof line.

7 Take the cut-out stable opening and fold back a ½in-wide strip along the base. This strip will eventually be glued on to the stable.

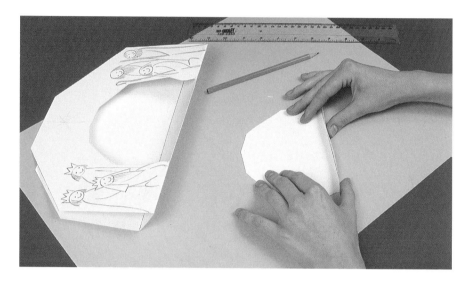

8 Draw a picture of the nativity family on the cut-out stable opening.

9 Cut around your picture of the nativity family. Be sure to leave the folded strip on the base.

10 Color the stable inside and out. Color the nativity family, too.

11 Glue the base of the nativity family picture behind the stable opening.

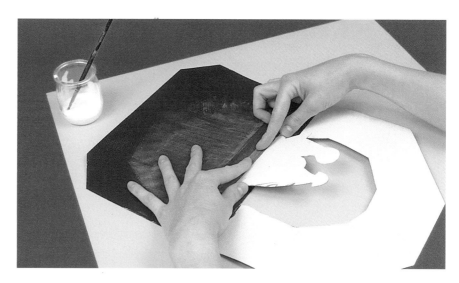

12 Squeeze or brush a line of glue along the roof edges.

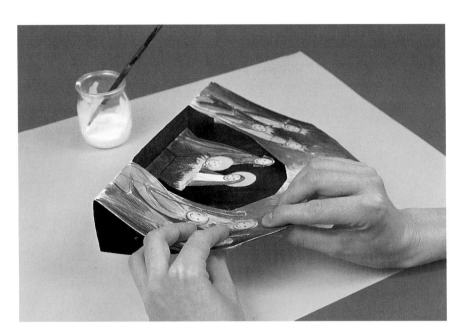

13 Stick the front and back roof edges together.

14 The paper nativity crib is now complete and ready to use at Christmastime.

The peepshow is a magical world sealed in a box. The only view into it is a small peephole. From writings and paintings we know that children enjoyed peepshows as far back as the 18th century. When making your own peepshow, think of the scene you would like to create: a jungle, a haunted house, a magician's cave, an underwater world or some other magical setting.

You will need a medium-sized cardboard box, scissors or a trimming knife, thin white cardboard or thick paper, a pencil, a ruler, paints and paintbrushes (or inks, felt-tipped pens or crayons), glue, colored cellophane or tissue paper, and masking tape.

1 Cut a peephole (about ½in radius) in the center of one end of the box. Use a washer, button or coin as a size guide.

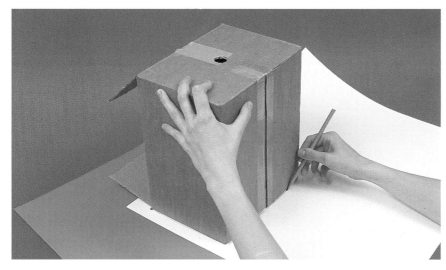

2 Stand the box on its end, lay it on the cardboard or paper and draw around it.

3 Draw a ¾in-wide frame around the shape of the box end. Repeat steps 2 and 3 twice more. (You need a total of three box end shapes with frames – one for the background, one for the foreground and a third for the middle distance.)

4 Cut out the three complete shapes and cut off the corners.

5 Fold in the edges of the shapes, just inside the original lines.

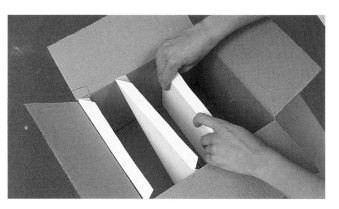

6 Place the three shapes inside the box and check that they fit.

7 Remove the shape furthest from the peephole and draw your background design on it.

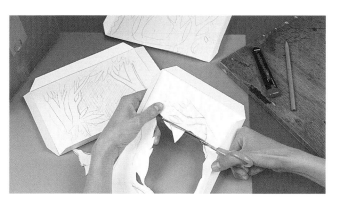

8 Design the foreground and center pieces, too. Each of these must have an area cut away in the middle to give a view through to the background.

9 Now color the three pieces. Keep putting the scenery into place and peeping through the hole, to make sure you are getting the effects you want.

10 Glue the scenery into place in the box. The best position for each piece will be found by looking through the peephole.

11 Cut a large hole in the top of the box to let light in.

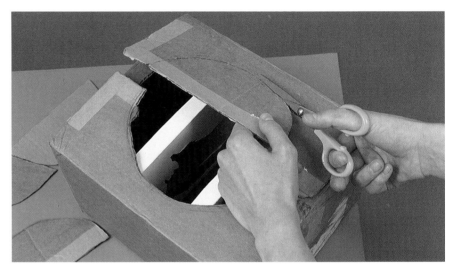

12 Cover the hole with colored cellophane or tissue paper. Secure the covering in position with glue or masking tape. You can decorate the box, if you like, by painting it or by covering it with colored wrapping paper. (Remember not to cover the two holes!)

13 A view into a
completed peepshow.

You will need two sheets of paper (8½ x 11in in size), a pencil, a ruler, scissors or a trimming knife, a pair of compasses, paints and paintbrushes (or inks, felt-tipped pens or crayons), and a brass paper fastener.

1 Find the center of one of the sheets of paper by drawing four identical rectangles. Make a small hole where the four lines cross.

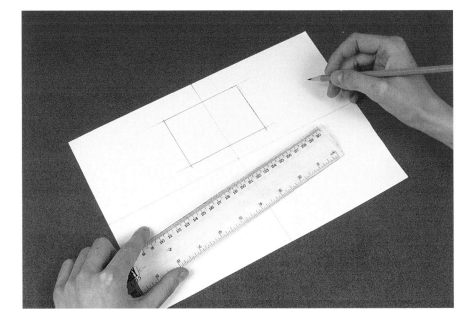

2 Draw a fifth rectangle, 3½in wide x 2½in high, on the paper. Its base should be ¾in above the central hole, and it should be positioned so that the vertical line from the central hole runs through the center of the rectangle.

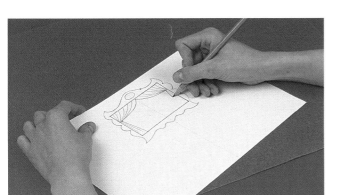

3 This rectangle will be the stage opening or "proscenium." Decorate it with a frame and drawn curtains.

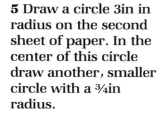

4 Cut out the stage opening, leaving the stage curtains in position.

5 Draw a circle 3in in radius on the second sheet of paper. In the center of this circle draw another, smaller circle with a ¾in radius.

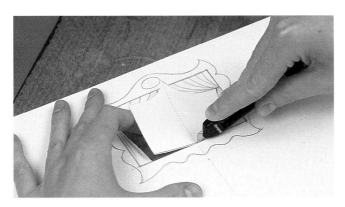

6 Cut out the outer circle.

7 Working from the edge of the smaller circle outward, draw pictures of the characters from the play you have chosen to illustrate. These characters could be in dramatic positions to make the story exciting.

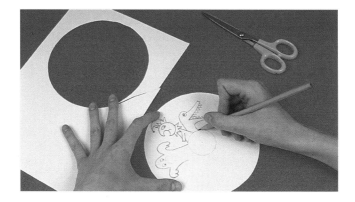

8 Color the booth, stage opening and circle of characters.

9 Place the disk behind the stage opening and join it to the booth by pushing the brass paper fastener through the central hole on the booth and through the center of the small circle on the disk.

10 Fold the sides of the booth back, making sure that there is enough room for the disk to turn easily.

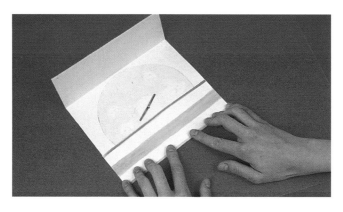

11 Your stage and characters are
now ready for your story drama.

Tinsel portraits were very popular in the 18th and early 19th centuries. They were collected, much as pictures of movie or television stars or sports personalities are collected today. Your local museum may have examples for you to look at.

You will need a sheet of paper, a pencil, paints and paintbrushes (or inks, felt-tipped pens or crayons), scraps of metallic paper, scissors, a hole punch (useful but not essential), glue, silver and/or gold metallic ink pens, sequins, and feathers.

1 Draw a pantomime or circus character on the sheet of paper. Draw the figure in a dramatic pose.

2 Color the figure. Add a little background detail to give a feeling of the setting in which the character might be found.

3 Smooth out the scraps of metallic paper and cut out the shapes needed to decorate the figure. If you have a hole punch, punch out some pieces to use in the decoration.

4 Glue the shiny paper shapes to your drawing.

5 Final details can be added with the silver or gold metallic ink pens. Sequins and feathers can also be used as decoration.

6 A completed tinsel portrait.

You will need an old shoe box, a pencil, a ruler, scissors or a trimming knife, poster or tempera paints, paintbrushes, scraps of metallic paper, and glue.

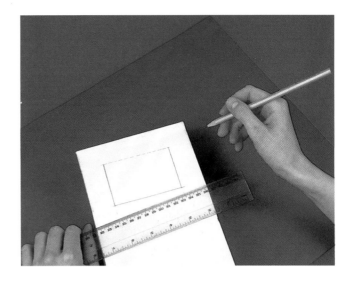

1 Draw a rectangle 3½in wide x 2¼in high on the bottom of the shoe box, about 1⅛in in from one of the short edges. Position the rectangle so that there is an equal amount of space on either side between the edges of the rectangle and the long edges of the box. This rectangle will be the stage opening, or proscenium.

2 (Above) Cut along the sides and bottom of the proscenium, leaving the top edge attached.

3 Bend the top edge back to form a curtain for the stage.

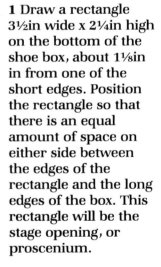

4 Paint the box and decorate it with shapes cut from the scraps of metallic paper.

5 Your theater is now ready. All it needs are puppets. Use finger puppets, or try some paper cone figures (see pages 25-27).

You will need sheets of thick paper or thin cardboard, a pencil, a pair of compasses, scissors, glue, and paints and paintbrushes (or inks, felt-tipped pens or crayons).

1 Draw a circle with a 2½in radius on a sheet of paper. Using the same central point draw a second, smaller circle with a 1¼in radius.

2 Cut around the outer circle, then cut out the inner circle, leaving a ring of paper.

3 Cut the ring in half. Roll one half around your index finger until it sits firmly in place when you move your finger, then glue down the ends to form a cone shape. Repeat this process, making one cone for each character you need.

4 Draw your characters on paper or cardboard, then color them. Each character should be 2-2¼in high.

5 Cut out all the characters and glue them onto the paper cones. Color the cones to match.

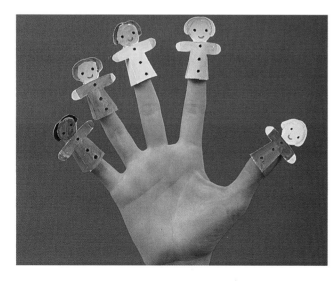

6 The index finger is probably the easiest finger to use for your paper cone figures, but if you need more figures on stage try using your other fingers as well. (You may have to make the cones different sizes, to fit your other fingers.)

7 You can now stage a show using your paper cone figures and the shoe box booth (see pages 23-24).

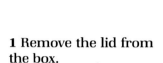

You will need a cardboard box (shoe boxes are strong and a good size), scissors, a ruler, a pencil, a trimming knife, poster or tempera paints, and paintbrushes.

1 Remove the lid from the box.

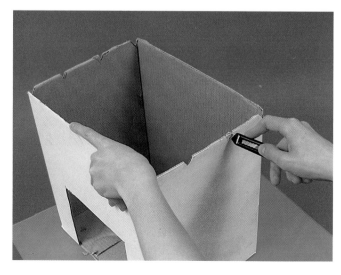

2 Make a stage opening, or proscenium, on the front of the box. Cut out the proscenium.

3 Cut triangular grooves along the top side edges of the box. Cut one groove close to the front of the box for the curtain, one at the back for the backdrop and one or two in between for scenery or center drops.

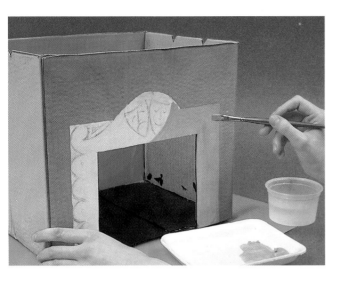

4 Draw and paint the proscenium, back wall and stage floor.

5 This toy theater is ready for scenery and puppets (see pages 30-38).

You will need your toy theater (see pages 28-29), four wooden dowels or skewer sticks, a cardboard box (the same size as the one you used for your toy theater), a trimming knife, scissors, masking tape, a pencil, poster or tempera paints, paintbrushes, and a reading lamp or flashlight.

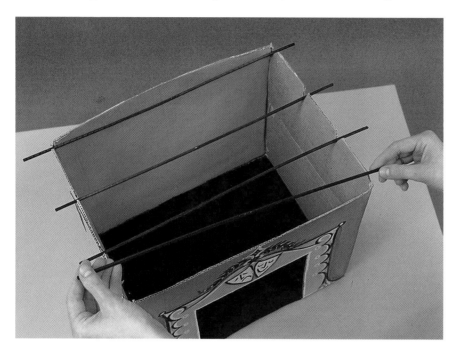

1 Place a dowel across each set of grooves.

2 Cut up the cardboard box. You will need the four box sides.

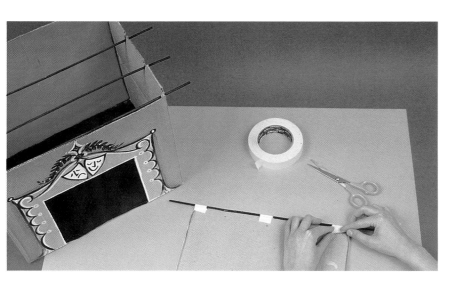

3 Using masking tape, stick one of the wide box sides to the rod at the back of the toy theater. This will be the backdrop.

4 Secure the other wide box side to the front rod. This will be the front curtain.

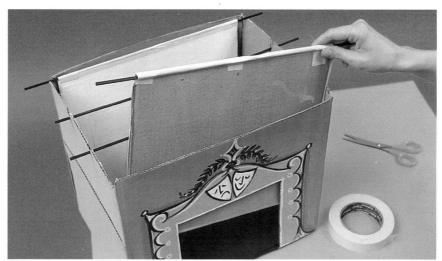

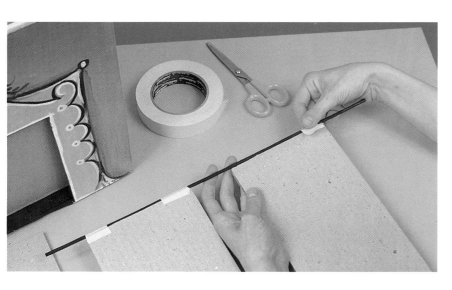

5 Cut the two remaining box sides in half lengthwise and, using masking tape, attach two to each of the center rods. Place each piece as far apart as possible, so that they touch the side walls on the inside of the theater. These two pieces are called the "wings," or "side masking."

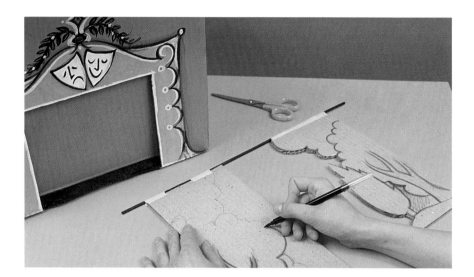

6 Draw scenery on the wing pieces. Keep the outside edges straight but cut out the inside edges to form buildings, trees or whatever scenery your play requires.

7 Draw and paint the backdrop, wings and front curtain.

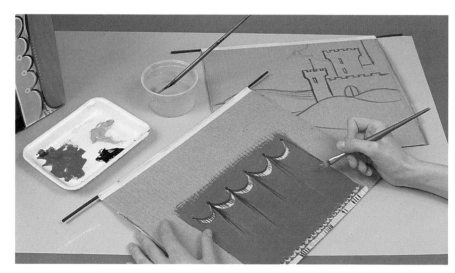

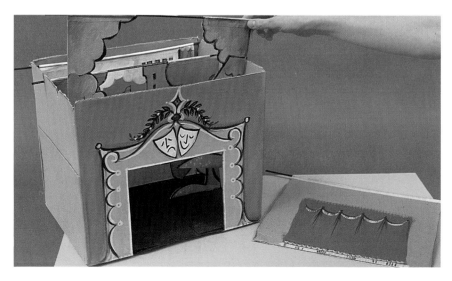

8 Put the finished wings and backdrop in position.

9 To light the stage, cut away the sides of the theater and use either a low-powered reading lamp or a flashlight. (You can also use the cut-out sides to make any figures worked by side rods enter and exit – see pages 36-38).

It is exciting to see changes of scenery during a show. This is done simply by designing other backdrops and wings which can be slipped in while the curtain is down.

You will need thin white cardboard, a pencil, scissors, dowel rods or skewer sticks, masking tape, poster or tempera paints, paintbrushes, wire, pliers, and a ruler.

Figures worked by rods from above

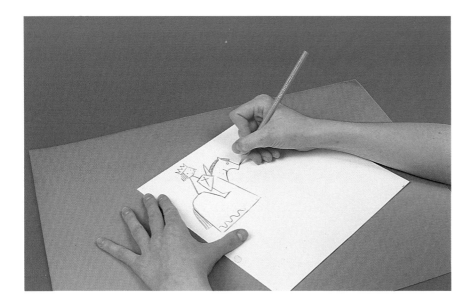

1 Draw figures on a piece of cardboard. Be sure that the figures are the right size for your theater.

2 Cut out the figures.

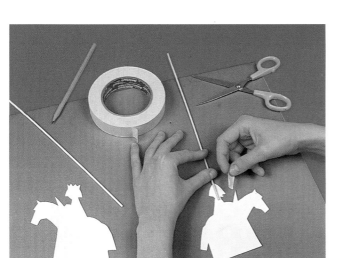

3 Attach a rod to each figure, using masking tape.

4 Paint the figures. Paint the fronts and backs so that you can turn the figures around.

5 Make small hooks from the wire and attach one to each rod with masking tape. The hooks need to be positioned so that when you hook the figures over the scenery rods that lie across the top of the theater, the figures stand up without being held and the bases of the figures lie just slightly above the stage floor.

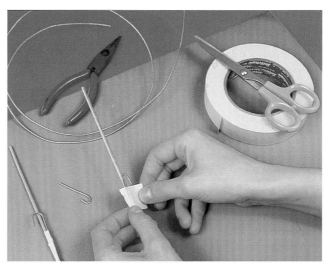

6 Here you see the puppets being operated from above. One person is able to perform a show single-handed.

Figures on side rods

7 Draw a line 1⅛in up from the bottom edge of another piece of cardboard.

8 Draw a series of figures with their feet touching this line. The area below the line will be the base on which the figures stand.

9 Cut out the figures, leaving the piece of blank cardboard below each figure attached. Fold back these base pieces and cut the edges at an angle, as shown.

10 Using masking tape, tape a rod to the base of each figure.

11 Paint the figures.

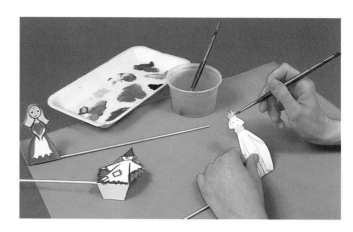

12 Here you see the figures in action. They are worked by side rods.

To light the stage, use either a low-powered reading lamp or a flashlight held from above or in front. To create different lighting effects, use colored gel filters over the lamp or cellophane over the flashlight.

WARNING: CELLOPHANE IS FLAMMABLE, SO DO NOT USE IT OVER AN ELECTRIC LIGHT BULB.

Stage

For the stage you will need a cardboard box, a pencil, scissors or a trimming knife, masking tape, poster or tempera paints, paintbrushes, a sheet of thin white paper, glue, and a reading lamp or flashlight.

1 Fold the front lid of the box back against one of the upright side lid pieces at an angle of about 45° and draw a line. Draw another line to meet the back corner, as shown. Do the same on the other side lid piece.

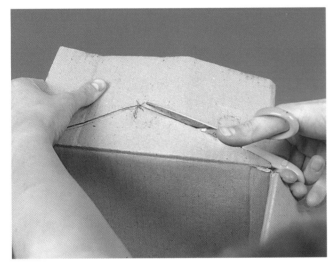

2 Cut along these lines.

3 Attach the front lid to the cut sides, using masking tape. This angled lid will act as a mask to hide the light from the audience's eyes.

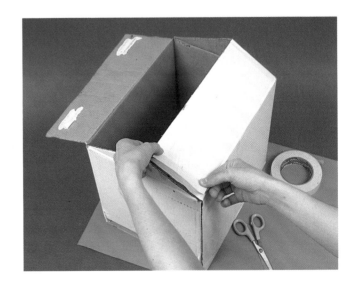

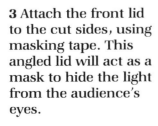

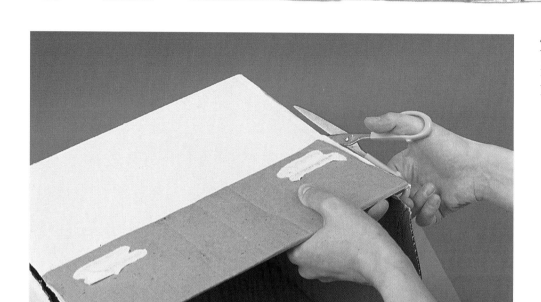

4 Cut out the whole back piece of the box, including the back lid piece.

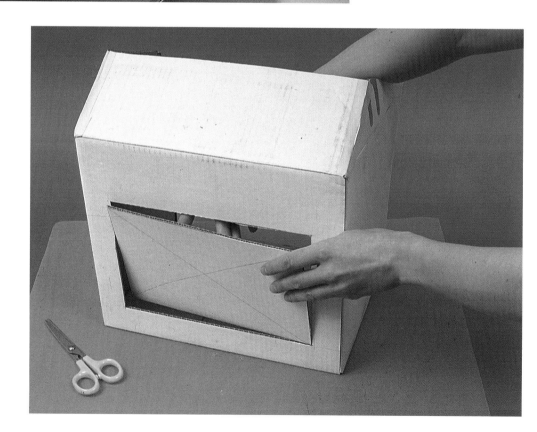

5 Draw and cut a proscenium on the front of the box.

6 Paint the box, either in one color or using a variety of colors and patterns.

7 Stick the sheet of thin white paper across the back of the proscenium, using glue or masking tape.

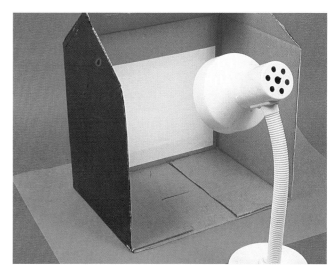

8 Position the reading lamp or flashlight so that it will shine onto the back of the screen.

Shadow figures

For the figures you will need stiff black paper or thin black cardboard, a white or light-colored pencil (to draw on the black paper or cardboard), scissors or a trimming knife, colored cellophane (or gel filters or tissue paper), glue, thin dowel rods or skewer sticks, Fun-Tac or masking tape, a reading lamp or flashlight, and brass paper fasteners.

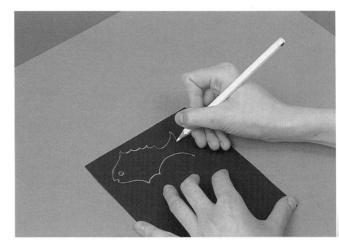

9 Draw figures on to the paper or cardboard.

10 Cut around the outlines of the figures.

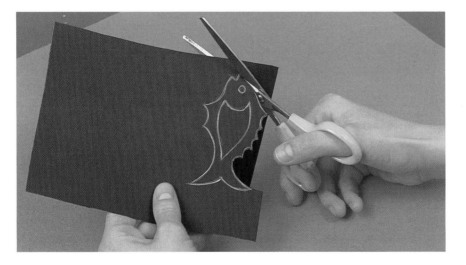

11 Cut out areas inside each figure.

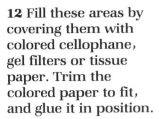

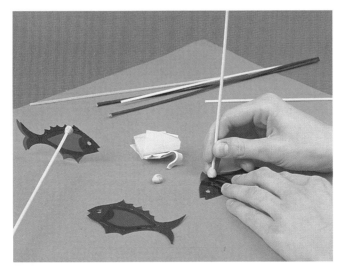

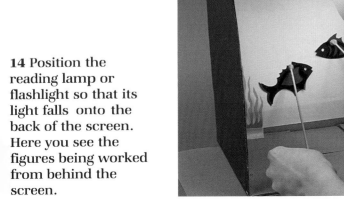

12 Fill these areas by covering them with colored cellophane, gel filters or tissue paper. Trim the colored paper to fit, and glue it in position.

13 Attach a dowel rod or skewer stick to each shadow figure using a small ball of Fun-Tac or a piece of masking tape.

14 Position the reading lamp or flashlight so that its light falls onto the back of the screen. Here you see the figures being worked from behind the screen.

15 This is the effect that the audience sees from the front.

16 Extra movement can be given to the figures by overlapping two pieces of cardboard and joining them with a brass paper fastener.

To create different effects and moods, use colored gel filters over the lamp or colored cellophane over the flashlight. WARNING: CELLOPHANE IS FLAMMABLE. DO NOT USE IT OVER AN ELECTRIC LIGHT BULB.

Ask a local theater group to save discarded pieces of gel filter for you, or order it from a theatrical supplier (see page 45).

Stationers and/or artists' materials shops will carry the majority of the items listed in this book. Special materials (or materials in large quantities) can be purchased through SAM FLAX INC., 39 West 19th St., New York, N. Y. 10011.

Lighting

You can buy packs of gel filter from: PRODUCTION ARTS LIGHTING INC., 636 11th Avenue, New York, N. Y. 10036.

Museums

If you would like to know more about toy theaters, visit or write to:

Museum of the City of New York
5th Avenue at 103rd St.
New York, N. Y. 10029
(by appointment only)

or

Pollocks Toy Museum
1 Scala Street
London W1
England

Both have a variety of theaters on display as well as theater scripts and books for sale.

If you are interested in studying theatrical portraits and "tinsel pictures," visit or write to:

Museum of the City of New York
5th Avenue at 103rd St.
New York, N. Y. 10029

or

New York Public Library
Lincoln Center/Theater Research
111 Amsterdam Avenue
New York, N. Y. 10023

A delightful form of entertainment known as "Juvenile Drama" or "Toy Theater" came into being at the beginning of the 19th century. In gaily painted cardboard theaters, miniature cut-out actors performed the favorite shows of the time for the enjoyment of all the family.

As well as being a wonderful home entertainment, these tiny theaters were also a record of the 19th-century theater. The drawings of the characters were often portraits of the actors and actresses of that time and the costumes and scenery were faithful copies of the work of the most popular and successful theatrical artists.

It is hard to say exactly how the idea of toy theater came about. Perhaps its beginnings lie in the 17th-century crib figures made of paper or in the peepshows of the 18th century. But its development can certainly be traced back to the theatrical souvenir sheets on sale at the end of the 18th and in the early years of the 19th centuries. These sheets were full-length drawings or "engravings" of the favorite theater characters of the time. The characters were shown in dramatic poses and the sheets were collected, much as photos of movie and television stars are collected today. The cost of a sheet was one penny for a plain (black and white) engraving or two pennies for a hand-colored version.

Once purchased, the sheets would be brought home, colored if necessary, then stuck on to cardboard and carefully cut out. They could be decorated, too, with small pieces of silk, velvet and metallic paper. When decorated, they became known as "tinsel portraits." Many happy evenings must have been spent by families coloring, cutting and decorating these lovely pictures.

At first each sheet showed only a single figure. Later, two or more characters from the shows were illustrated, as was the scenery. After the scenery came pictures of the theaters themselves, with engravings showing the beautifully decorated proscenium arch and the boxes near the stage where the rich ladies and gentlemen sat. Simple wooden structures to hold these

pictures were also sold.

The character pictures would be placed into little metal holders fastened to the ends of pieces of wire. To work a figure, the operator would hold the end of the wire and push the figure in from the wings (the sides of the stage hung with scenery to hide the entrances and exits of the actors). The same operator could also bring a figure or figures in from the opposite wings. To indicate which figure was speaking, the operator would move it back and forth in short, sharp movements. Very often the entire show was performed by a single person who would work all the actors, speak all the voices and make all the sound effects!

Scripts of plays began to be printed for use with these toy theaters. The original plays were not written for children, but it is likely that children enjoyed the idea of toy theater so much, plays and pantomimes soon came to be written especially for them.

So popular were these miniature theaters that more and more printers began to produce play scripts. There was great competition to be the first to bring out the script of the latest London show. After the first night of a show, printers would return to their workshops to draw, engrave and print, rushing to get the new sheets into the shops within a few days.

The craze for toy theaters lasted for over a hundred years but finally subsided in the 1930s. Many of the London printing shops were bombed during World War II and valuable engraving plates were destroyed. But toy theaters did not die out completely. Some of the old plates were later found, and a few specialist shops now sell reprinted versions complete with stages and scripts. And there are still toy theater enthusiasts in many parts of the world, who put on shows for the delight of their friends. A few travel the world, giving shows to the public. Keep a look-out – you may be lucky enough to see one of these delightful performances in your town.